Beyond Second Chances

New Beginnings for Forgiveness

Seven week program to achieve forgiveness, purpose and a more peaceful life

Caroline Rolleri MSW/ LSW/ Forgiveness Trainer

Beyond Second Chances was inspired to provide healing for the mind, body and spirit through the gift of forgiveness. It is my prayer that you will be empowered by Jesus to forgive and breakthrough any impossible situation. That through this program, you can heal and experience true love, purpose, peace, and joy.

"The Spirit of the Lord GOD is upon me; because the LORD hath anointed me to preach good tidings unto the meek; he hath sent me to bind up the brokenhearted, to proclaim liberty to the captives, and the opening of the prison to them that are bound;" (Isaiah 61:1)

"If we really want to love, we must learn how to forgive."-- Mother Theresa

Copyright 2015 by Carol Rolleri
ISBN-13: 978-0692540671 (Caroline J. Rolleri)
ISBN-10: 0692540679

All Scripture quotations, unless otherwise indicated, are taken from the Holy Bible; King James Version (KJV), which is public domain in the United States.

Disclaimer

The views expressed in the Beyond Second Chances training program are a guide to be considered when addressing issues of forgiveness. The program materials do not take the place of professional assistance in cases of abuse, violence, addiction, and extraordinary situations. Professional assistance should be pursued when an individual may be a danger to him/herself or others. Please note materials from the Beyond Second Chances training program are protected by copyright laws.

Acknowledgements

With great love, thankfulness and admiration, I would like to thank my family, friends and the great inspiration of my life: My wonderful Lord and Savior, Lord Jesus Christ. for giving me the ability to forgive and love. I would also like to thank the many friends who assisted with the editing, publishing, and help with making this book a reality.

"There is a terrible hunger for love. We all experience it in our lives. The pain and the loneliness, we must have the courage to recognize it. The poor you may have in your own family.
Find them... Love them. "

Quotes from Mother Theresa.

Table of Contents

Week One: Forgiveness — **Page 7**
Forgiveness
Misunderstandings about Forgiveness
Number One Action Step: Forgiveness

Week Two: Forgiving Others — **Page 10**
How can you forgive someone who has hurt you?
How can you forgive someone who died?
Breathing Forgiveness Method
What if someone does not want to forgive you?
Four step method to forgive others
Number Two Action Step: Forgiving Others

Week Three: How to forgive yourself — **Page 13**
Forgive Yourself
Forgive Yourself/Step One/ Belonging to God
Forgive yourself/Step Two/You are worthy
Number Three Action Step: Forgive Yourself

Week Four: Methods to experience forgiveness and avoid stress — **Page 15**
Forgiveness and Stress
Method One: The Mirror Method
Method Two: Music for the soul
Method Three: Pet therapy
Method Four: Read the Word of the Lord the Holy Bible
Scriptures on forgiveness for self and others
Scriptures on stress to encourage and calm the soul
Number Four Action Step: Methods to experience forgiveness and avoid stress

Week Five: Three Methods on how to communicate positively and achieve forgiveness. — **Page 18**
Communication is one of the keys to Forgiveness
Method One: How to communicate with women
Method Two: How to communicate with men
Method Three: The Love Languages
Number Five Action Step: Methods on how to communicate positively and achieve forgiveness.

Week Six: Forgiveness and Relationships: Family, Friendships and Co-workers   Page 22
Forgiveness and Relationships
Family Relationships
Method One: Forgiving Family Members
Would you put yourself in my shoes?
Method Two: Forgiving Family Members
Pray together
Forgiving and Friendships
Seven Qualities of Great Friendship
Forgiveness and Co-Workers
One Method of Co-worker forgiveness: Personality and Temperament
Number Six Action Step: Forgiveness, Relationships, Family, Friends and Co-Workers

Week Seven: Methods on how to achieve forgiveness of the mind, body, and spirit.   Page 27
Forgiveness and the mind
One Method of Forgiveness and the Mind
Inspirational Thoughts of Forgiveness for different areas of your life, spiritual, career, emotions, health, great goals, and finances.

Forgiveness and the body
Forgiveness gives you these health benefits for your body
Method One: To keep your body healthy as you continue to forgive: Eat Healthy
Method Two: To keep your body healthy as you continue to forgive: Exercise
Method Three: To keep our body healthy as you continue to forgive: Proper Rest
Forgiveness and the Spirit
One Method to Achieve Forgiveness in the Spirit: Prayer
Number Seven Action Step: Methods on how to achieve forgiveness of the mind, body, and spirit.
Forgiveness and the Mind
Forgiveness and the Body
Forgiveness and the Soul
How to Stay in Forgiveness
Closing thoughts on Beyond Second Chances
The Forgiveness House
Beyond Second Chances Website/ To Be Free /Weekly Blog/The Power of Forgiveness

Notes   **Page 35**
Bibliography   **Page 37**
About the Author   **Page 39**

Dear friend,

What started me on the journey towards forgiveness?

    I consider it a privilege and honor to have your time and attention as you seek to learn about love and forgiveness. As you take a seven week journey with the Lord, discover the freedom and joy you will find through forgiving others and yourself. Over the past ten years my passion has been to learn to live in forgiveness, and share with others the deep levels of peace that can be found in the body, mind, and spirit.

    I became fascinated with forgiveness while taking a course which asked the profound question: What is my purpose in life? As I prayed and searched my heart, I realized I was disappointed, discouraged, resentful and angry about a failed relationship with my ex-fiancé, and a job in which I felt mistreated and angry. Some other situations which have caused much resentment were unemployment, financial collapse, health issues, and being single. In addition, some friends and family who were emotionally unavailable during these difficult times further disappointed me. I felt very alone. The pain of these situations did not go away when I asked the Lord to help me forgive. The hurt and anger lingered on. I became very depressed and anxious. In tears, I cried out desperately to the Lord: "Please Lord, if you will change my situation, I will tell everyone how you healed my heart, mind and body". Within a year, the Lord opened doors that were shut for what had seemed like a lifetime. I asked the Lord to teach me to forgive. It was then that He helped me to forgive others.

    For most of my life I have struggled with anxiety and depression. Only when I truly forgave others did the anxiety and depression leave me. It was almost as if I was holding a backpack full of heavy rocks. When I forgave from my heart, I experienced a new life in Christ. I experienced the freedom that is spoken of in the Lord. I truly want to love and forgive others. My desire for you is to restore broken relationships with the Lord, loved ones, family, friends, co-workers and the community at large. Learning to truly be able to forgive, from your heart, will help you to forgive anyone – even your enemies. It is only through my pain and suffering that I have found the true grace of the Lord.

Blessings, Love, and Forgiveness
Caroline Rolleri, Forgiveness Trainer
Beyond Second Chances

Week One: Forgiveness

Forgiveness

The American Heritage Dictionary references forgiveness as, "letting go of past grudges or lingering anger against a person or persons." Forgiveness is a process, it takes time for the pain and hurt to diminish. There is no simple or easy way to let go of resentment. It will definitely reappear. Yet, it is up to the individual to continue to forgive, so that the resentment does not continue to erode the body, soul and mind.

Jesus Our Lord talked about forgiveness when He was asked how to pray. "This, then, is how you should pray:

"After this manner therefore pray ye: Our Father which art in heaven, Hallowed be thy name.

Thy kingdom come, Thy will be done in earth, as it is in heaven.

Give us this day our daily bread.

And forgive us our debts, as we forgive our debtors.

And lead us not into temptation, but deliver us from evil: For thine is the kingdom, power and the glory, forever. Amen.

For if ye forgive men their trespasses, your heavenly Father will also forgive you.

But if ye forgive not men their trespasses, neither will your Father forgive your trespasses." (Matthew 6:9-15)

Before I forgave, I felt as if I was carrying around a backpack filled with rocks. Resentment was my constant companion; in the store, at my job, and even in church. When I forgave, I was set free. It felt as if I had let go of the extra weight of resentment I had been carrying around.

As an example of my experience of forgiveness, l will use a former manager to demonstrate the power of forgiveness. This person will be named Negative.

Believe me, we clashed. Due to Negative's pessimistic attitude and my optimistic attitude, we clashed like oil and water. It was difficult, to say the least, working on a daily basis with someone who was as negative as my former manager. Negative was critical, ignored me in meetings, and on a consistent basis hardly ever had a positive thing to say about my work. My manager viewed life on the gloomy side. When I would say good morning, 'negative' would ask, 'What is good about today?' This type of behavior wore me down. Being positive is courteous and helps to improve morale. Working together in a friendly environment and being cooperative helps the work get done in a more simplistic manner. Isn't that what everyone wants?

Forgiveness did help keep me from thinking about the horrible things 'negative' did during work, and how it affected my time away from work. Before I was able to forgive 'negative', I would dread going to work because of the atmosphere that had been created. After I forgave from my heart, I thought, "Why should I allow so much control over my life." Who is anyone to allow it? I thought, 'What a waste of time and energy. I want to spend the limited time I have at work, and on the weekends, in a more positive manner." When I forgave my manager, I was able to think of him in the present rather than the past. I realized that the past was gone and I began to concentrate on the moment at hand, and the work I had to complete that day.

When I forgave, I could focus on myself and realize how I may have contributed to some of the problems. I stopped blaming my manager. I needed to change some of the ways I did my work. My manager pointed out I should be more organized and use better time management skills. Looking back, I did need to improve these skills. Presently I am more teachable and do not always have to be right. I had to change my attitude and realize maybe he was trying to be helpful.

Did I misread my manager? I realized I could not change others. It is enough trying to take care of myself in this life. Through this experience I have learned to accept people for who they are, and love them unconditionally. Love the person and not their behavior. Let the Lord Judge people and their actions. Pray for them. Forgiveness is extending a hand of peace and being open and honest with others. The Holy Bible states "Therefore if thou bring thy gift to the altar, and there remembers that thy brother hath ought against thee; Leave there thy gift before the altar, and go thy way; first be reconciled to thy brother, and then come and offer thy gift." (Matthew 5:23-24)

"Put on therefore, as the elect of God, holy and beloved, bowels of mercies, kindness, humbleness of mind, meekness, longsuffering; Forbearing one another, and forgiving one another, if any man have a quarrel against any: even as Christ forgave you, so also do And above all these things put on charity, which is the bond of perfectness. .And let the peace of God rule in your hearts, to the also ye are called in one body; and be ye thankful." (Col 3: 12-15).

Another experience of the beauty of forgiveness was in my first job as a social worker. I worked with a woman who refused to train me as a new employee. She was critical, gossiped about me, and was unfriendly. I was very upset with her and prayed for almost 8 months for Jesus to help me to forgive her. I was praying for Jesus' blessing upon her life. I did speak to her privately and asked her what I could do to make things work better between us.

At our meeting, I said, "After all, we work together 40 hours a week. At least we can try to get along." As we spoke, she told me she was upset because she thought I was going to steal her job from her. She then apologized for her behavior. After the discussion we became friends. The power of forgiveness is real! Shortly after this situation, I was rewarded with a new job that paid a lot more than I had been making. In addition, I liked this job better.

Forgiveness can benefit you in every area of your life as well. Tell yourself, 'I will forgive because it will only hurt me, not them.' The people who you are resentful towards most likely are not thinking about you at all. Don't waste your precious time worrying.

Misunderstandings about Forgiveness

You may want to reconcile with another person, yet they are not willing. It is recommended to pray for them and let the Lord change their heart. In the meantime, ask the Lord to help you to show them love. Let the Lord change them in his way, and in his timing. Forgiveness does not mean you were not hurt. **To pretend you do not feel hurt will only prevent you from confronting your resentment. Healing will happen when you can admit you are in pain.**

If an individual is abusive, healthy boundaries and safety are important. Sometimes, being removed from a situation for the health and welfare of the family and individuals affected is the best solution. Please pray that the Lord will lead you to the appropriate help.

Number One Action Step: Forgiveness

Please pray for your heart to be open to the Holy Spirit and his leading. Ask yourself, "What is the goal of taking this program? Think of all the people in your life you have, or have not, forgiven. Find a trusted family member, friend, counselor, or clergy who will mentor you as you follow through with this program, if you are serious about forgiveness.

Pray to Jesus and mention to the Lord, "I accept whatever the answer and outcome. I choose to follow you. I surrender all to you. Help me to forgive from my heart. I cannot do this on my own I need your help."

Week Two: Forgiving Others

How can you forgive someone who has hurt you?

Our Lord Jesus taught about the importance of forgiveness. Forgiveness will help us to forgive those who hurt us. These words speak the truth about forgiveness. "And forgive us our sins; for we also forgive every one that is indebted to us. And lead us not into temptation; but deliver us from evil." (Luke 11:4)

How can you forgive someone who has died?

What if someone is deceased and you want to forgive them? One method is to visit the cemetery where they are buried, and tell them in a letter what they did to hurt you. Ask the Lord to help you forgive them. Say to them, "I choose to forgive you and let the Lord be your judge". What you can do is then rip up the letter and place it in a waste paper basket. You may also bring along a trusted friend or family member to help with the forgiveness process. When your bitter thoughts return, remind yourself of the day you forgave that individual, and tell yourself 'I cannot change the past and I only have today. I cannot waste another precious moment, there is only now.'

Another method of forgiveness I learned in college is the Empty Chair Method, a technique used with Gestalt therapy. Place an empty chair in a room and pretend the person you want to forgive is in the chair. Talk to the empty chair as if the person you would like to forgive is sitting there. Express your hurt, anger or disappointment with the invisible person.

Ask the Lord for wisdom and forgiveness toward this individual.

Breathing Forgiveness Method

Breathe in the good and breathe out the bitterness. Think of that person as someone who the Lord loves. He or she is human, and we all make mistakes. Say to yourself, 'I will let Jesus judge. I know that I too have made mistakes.' In your quiet time with the Lord, ask Him: 'What lessons can I learn from this? What can I teach others by this experience?' Pray to Jesus for His answer.

What if someone does not want to forgive you?

Be the peacemaker. Reach out in love and ask for forgiveness. If the person does not want to reconcile, kindly ask the person what happened. Is there a way that we can make things better between us? You cannot force anyone to forgive, as each of us has a free will. Continue praying that the other person's heart will be softened. Jesus will answer in his own time.

The Four Step method to forgive others
What if another does not want to forgive you and you keep trying to make peace?

Step One: Pray for the person as the bible commands. In (Mathew 5:44) it states, "But I say unto you, Love your enemies, bless them that curse you, do good to them that hate you, and pray for them which despitefully use you, and persecute you."

During your prayer time, ask the Lord to understand the other person. You may or may not want to speak to the person about your problems with them. Give them time and space to cool off, especially since you truly do not know what they are going through. They may have health, family, marriage, financial, work, or addiction issues which you are unaware of. Give them the benefit of the doubt. Perhaps the Lord can use you to show love to this person. Remember, you can't change others or their behaviors, only your attitude toward them.

Step Two: If you are led by God to call them to speak with them, call. Allow them to talk without interruption and try to understand them. Tell them what you think they have said. Make sure you understand them and they understand you. Many times a misunderstanding can cause anger and hurt, and become the reason for not forgiving others. Being the peacemaker can open the lines of communication and breakdown invisible walls.

Step Three: If after step two they do not call or write, continue to pray for this person's heart to be softened. Call or write a letter stating that you would like to talk to them if you have offended them. Tell them you are sorry for your part in the conflict. You can be the peacemaker. Extend your hand in the name of peace. Make sure that you keep in mind, 'Life is too short.' Remember, many people like to think of themselves as right, regardless of their part in a situation. I believe the following humble behavior will break the most stubborn individual; Send them a gift and tell them something that you appreciate about them. Gifts can breakdown the most hardened heart

Step Four: If they continue to resist your attempt to restore the relationship, pray for them to soften their heart. Send them a card for their birthday and be there by calling on the phone, or sending a card when they are grieving. When the Lord inspires you, do a random act of kindness for this person.

We cannot force ourselves on someone else since we all have a free will. If they are meant to be back in our life, it will happen. If not, always remember the good times. The Lord for this season may close those doors for now or forever. Trust in the Lord's timing that he will work it all out for our good. Remember to do your part and the Lord will take care of the rest. We cannot control people.

Number Two Action Step: Forgiving Others

How has not forgiving others had an impact on your significant relationships? Think in terms of how the offended person may view the situation. Look at it as if you were in their shoes and experienced the world the way in which they may have. Please be compassionate and merciful to them when you do this, even though it may be difficult.

Week Three: How to Forgive Yourself

Forgive Yourself

Many of us have made mistakes in our lives, such as adultery, addictions, stealing, jealousy, envy, constant fighting in marriage, and poor parenting, to name just a few. Due to our undesirable behaviors we feel guilt, rejection, loneliness, anxiety and depression, even after we decide to change our behaviors and apologize. We never think we can be good enough. It's as if we are constantly thinking in our head, "I'm a loser. There will never be a second chance in life for me."

I have found great news! There are two steps which can help you forgive yourself; belonging to God and knowing you are worthy. Dr. Charles Stanley discussed these areas in the broadcast "Victory Over Rejection."

Forgive Yourself Step One: Belonging to God

Some of us tell ourselves we will never fit in or be accepted by others because of our past mistakes. We continue to feel like the outsiders looking in. We tell ourselves that we are not to be forgiven. Isn't it tremendous to know that no matter what the circumstances are in life, you belong, are accepted, and are not condemned by Jesus? The following Bible scriptures are very powerful and allow you to experience belonging to God;

"Among whom are ye also the called of Jesus Christ."(Romans 1:6.)

"There is therefore now no condemnation to them which are in Christ Jesus, who walk not after the flesh, but after the Spirit..For the law of the Spirit of life in Christ Jesus hath made me free from the law of sin and death."(Romans 8: 1-2)

For today let us celebrate that you are not condemned, and can now live free in Christ. **We are meant to be accepted, not rejected.**

Forgive Yourself Step Two: You are worthy

When you wake up in the morning and tell yourself there is no way I can be forgiven for what I have done, God tells you differently. God forgives you. In the Holy Bible it states, "To him give all the prophets witness, that through his name whosoever believeth in him shall receive remission of sins." (Acts 10:43.)

"All unrighteousness is sin: and there is a sin not unto death."(1 John 5:17)

"If we confess our sins, he is faithful and just to forgive us our sins, and to cleanse us from all unrighteousness." (1 John 1:9)

Number Three Action Step: Forgive yourself

This week take 15 minutes of prayer time each day and ask the Lord to reveal areas of your life where you need to forgive yourself. Keep a journal and diary of the insight you are given. See if you find a pattern of rejection, shame, guilt or anger towards yourself, and ask the Lord to heal your heart. You can overcome guilt, shame, grudges and resentment of yourself through the power of forgiveness. For further emphasis, refer to Romans 8:1-2.

If the reader has difficulty with Action Step Three, please remember the following: The views expressed in the Beyond Second Chances training program are a guide to be considered when addressing issues of forgiveness. The training materials do not take the place of professional assistance in cases of abuse, violence, addiction, and extraordinary situations. Professional assistance should be pursued when an individual may be a danger to him/herself or others.

Week Four: Methods to experience forgiveness and avoid stress

Forgiveness and Stress

Many times we experience stress due to feelings of anger, bitterness, and resentment which occur when we do not forgive ourselves or others. This week we will discuss four methods to use when we would like to give forgiveness, rather than receive stress. Use these four methods to experience the true inner peace that can be found in forgiveness.

Method One: The Mirror Method

This method can help take away stress and tap into Our Lord's presence and forgiveness. It takes about 5 minutes a day and is more relaxing in a quiet place. Please listen to relaxing music and experience quiet during your special time. Place a full length mirror in front of you and state to yourself the following, "Lord I give this day to you. I offer it for forgiveness, self-esteem, stress and your love."

Take your hand and touch your head /tell yourself, "I have the mind of Christ", as it states in the Holy Bible "For who hath known the mind of the Lord, that he may instruct him? but we have the mind of Christ."(1 Corinthians 2:16)

Touch your eyes and tell yourself "I will see what the Lord would like me to see in my world." As Mother Theresa stated, "I see Christ in everyone." Breathe, and breathe in goodness, forgiveness and love. Breathe out grudges, hopelessness, selfishness, stress, gossip, slander, and unkindness.

Touch your mouth and say, "My dear brothers and sisters, take note of this": "Everyone should be quick to listen, slow to speak and slow to become angry." "Wherefore, my beloved brethren, let every man be swift to hear, slow to speak, slow to wrath."(James 1:19)

Stretch out the palms of your hands and say:

My hands will be used to work the gifts of the Lord, to forgive and love.

My legs will walk to places where someone would need help, to give joy, peace, love and forgiveness."

Method Two: Music for the soul

After listening to music and singing calming soothing music, we are more calm and able to make better decisions on how to forgive, and react to the person who offended us, in a loving way. Scripture that talks about the power of music, "And the ransomed of the Lord shall return, and come to Zion with songs and everlasting joy upon their heads: they shall obtain joy and gladness, and sorrow and sighing shall flee away." (Isaiah 35:10)

The benefits of music to forgive and calm our soul can be found in music therapy as well. In the article, "Music and your Body: How music affects us and why music therapy promotes health" Elizabeth Scott, MA Stress Management expert, states the following:

"Those who practice music therapy are finding a benefit in using music to help cancer patients, children with ADD, and others, and even hospitals are beginning to use music and music therapy to help with pain management, to help ward off depression, to promote movement, to calm patients, to ease muscle tension, and for many other benefits that music and music therapy can bring."

Method Three: Pet therapy

Our pets bring us much joy, laughter and love. They give us unconditional love. They are precious with their beautiful tapestry of colors, and are truly one of God's greatest gifts to us. Passages in the bible that describe animals are listed below. When we are stressed about people and how they will not forgive us, we can find peace with our furry little friends, which the Lord made to bring us peace and comfort.

"A righteous man regarded the life of his beast: but the tender mercies of the wicked are cruel." (Proverbs 12:10)

"Behold the fowls of the air: for they sow not, neither do they reap, nor gather into barns; yet your heavenly Father feeded them. Are ye not much better than they?"(Mathew 6:26)

There is research provided of the benefits of pet therapy to reduce stress and help us to love and then forgive others. According to the article, Pets for Depression and Health, Web MD, "Pets offer an unconditional love that can be very helpful to people with depression, says Ina Cook, MD, a psychiatrist and director of the Depression Research and Clinic Program at UCLA. Studies show that animals can reduce tension and improve mood. Along with treatment pets can help some people with mild to moderate depression feel better".

Other benefits of pet therapy would include mental stimulation .According to the article, The Benefits We Experience When Pets (Animals) Are Beside Us, "Mental stimulation occurs because of increased communication with other people, recalled memories, and the entertainment provided by the animals. In situations that are depressing or institutional, the presence of the animals serves to brighten the atmosphere, increasing amusement, laughter, and play. These positive distractions may help to decrease people's feelings of isolation or alienation."

Method Four: Read the Word of the Lord, the Holy Bible

The Holy Bible gives hope to those who would like to forgive and are experiencing bitterness, anger, stress and. resentment. The Holy Bible provides wisdom, direction and answers to life's difficulties and challenges. Please note the Bible scriptures that offer encouragement on forgiveness and stress.

Scriptures on forgiveness for self and others

"Who hath delivered us from the power of darkness, and hath translated us into the kingdom of his dear Son: In whom we have redemption through his blood, even the forgiveness of sins." (Colossians 1:13-14)

"For if ye forgive men their trespasses, your heavenly Father will also forgive you."(Matthew 6:14)

"Let all bitterness, and wrath, and anger, and clamour, and evil speaking, be put away from you, with all malice: And be ye kind one to another, tenderhearted, forgiving one another, even as God for Christ's sake hath forgiven you." (Ephesians 4:31-32)

Scriptures on Stress to encourage and calm the soul; "Be strong and of a good courage, fear not, nor be afraid of them: for the Lord thy God, he it is that doth go with thee; he will not fail thee, nor forsake thee." (Deuteronomy 31:6)

Scriptures on stress to encourage; "For I know the thoughts that I think toward you, saith the Lord, thoughts of peace, and not of evil, to give you an expected end. Then shall ye call upon me, and ye shall go and pray unto me, and I will hearken unto you... And ye shall seek me, and find me, when ye shall search for me with all your heart. And I will be found of you, saith the Lord: and I will turn away your captivity, and I will gather you from all the nations, and from all the places whither I have driven you, saith the Lord; and I will bring you again into the place whence I caused you to be carried away captive." (Jeremiah 29:11-14)

Number Four Action Step: Methods to experience forgiveness and avoid stress.

Spend time daily thanking the Lord for who He is. Find a quiet place and pray for the Lord to show you how to relax and just listen to the Holy Spirit. Use these methods consistently and much stress can be reduced, and forgiveness can occur in your silent time. Please take time to take care of your spiritual man or woman. Please keep a journal of how the Lord speaks to you in these precious, quiet times.

Week Five: Three Methods on how to communicate positively and achieve forgiveness

Communication is one of the keys to Forgiveness

From the cradle to the grave we communicate all the time, much of which seems to cause great problems and misunderstandings. Very often we are rushed in our world and can miss what others are trying to communicate to us. According to Gary Harris, in the article "Listen More and Speak Less- 5 Steps to become a better listener; "As hard as it is to listen effectively, it is still vitally important. Immediately after we listen to someone, we only recall about 50% of what they said. Long-term, we only remember 20% of what we hear."

This type of miscommunication can lead to a misunderstanding, which can then result in hurt feelings, being offended, rejection, anger, bitterness, and ultimately not wanting to forgive others. It is very important to learn how to communicate effectively. Learning great communication skills can help to avoid having to apologize for insensitive words and avoid not forgiving in our hearts. This week we will learn what communication is, how women and men communicate differently, and the five love languages. Let us apply these skills daily in our lives to have more loving and forgiving relationships.

According to the Merriam-Webster dictionary, communication is defined as "the act or process of using words, sounds, signs, or behaviors to express or exchange information, or to express your ideas, thoughts, feelings, etc., to someone else, or a message that is given to someone (i.e.; a letter or telephone call, etc.)."The Bible has a similar thought on how to communicate. One of my favorite scriptures, which I like to live by, is "Wherefore, my beloved brethren, let every man be swift to hear, slow to speak, slow to wrath:" (James 1:19)

Living the scripture as (James 1:19) indicates, will help us to communicate in a more loving manner in order to avoid miscommunication and arguments. How many relationships, marriages, families, friendships, jobs, and reputations were destroyed by the words we said, or did not say. Just think, some families do not talk to each other, carrying grudges for generations because of something said years before. Let us be the peacemakers, not the people who bring destruction. All these words are controlled by this little body part called the tongue. The tongue, which is a very small part of the body, can ruin or encourage. James 3; 4-14 describes the power of our words. "Behold also the ships, which though they be so great, and are driven of fierce winds, yet are they turned about with a very small helm, whithersoever the governor listeth.

Even so the tongue is a little member, and boasteth great things. Behold, how great a matter a little fire kindleth! And the tongue is a fire, a world of iniquity: so is the tongue among our members, that it defileth the whole body, and setteth on fire the course of nature; and it is set on fire of hell. For every kind of beasts, and of birds, and of serpents, and of things in the sea, is tamed, and hath been tamed of mankind: But the tongue can no man tame; it is an unruly evil, full of deadly poison. Therewith bless we God, even the Father; and therewith curse we men, which are made after the similitude of God. Out of the same mouth proceedeth blessing and cursing. My brethren, these things ought not so to be. Doth a fountain send forth at the same place sweet water and bitter? Can the fig tree, my brethren, bear olive berries? either a vine, figs? so can no fountain both yield salt water and fresh. Who is a wise man and endued with knowledge among you? let him shew out of a good conversation his works with meekness of wisdom. But if ye have bitter envying and strife in your hearts, glory not, and lie not against the truth."

"And be ye kind one to another, tenderhearted, forgiving one another, even as God for Christ's sake hath forgiven you." (Ephesians 4:32)

Let us think before we speak. Ask yourself; is it necessary, helpful in any way, and is the timing right.

Method One: How to communicate with women.

Please Love Me

Women communicate in a different manner than men. According to an article by Graham Reid, "How to Love a Woman", he highlighted the importance of telling a woman that you love her. In addition, he recommended not living in the past. Most importantly, he advised men to give their love to a woman, and to pay attention to her.

When women are not shown love, they feel unwanted, unloved, and unappreciated. These feeling can cause resentment resulting in not forgiving. The words we say, or do not say, can make or break a relationship. Women need to be spoken to and to hear that they are beautiful, as opposed to being ignored. Women cannot live on "I love you" once every year for a lifetime.

There is a story about a man whose wife died without him ever telling her that he loved her. He thought it was a waste of time. She asked him during her lifetime to tell her that he loved her, and he continually refused. Instead, he waited to tell her that he loved her at the cemetery site. This foolish husband cried. How sad. Why wait?

Method Two: How to communicate with men.

How do you think men communicate? Respect

According to the Merriam Webster encyclopedia, respect is described as" a feeling of admiring someone or something that is good, valuable, important, etc.: a feeling or understanding that someone or something is important, serious, etc., and should be treated in an appropriate way. : to consider worthy of high regard: esteem ,to refrain from interfering with please respect their privacy: to have reference to concern".

Respect is a man's language and it motivates him, according to a book by Eggerich, titled, "Love and Respect." "Men need to be shown that they matter and are important. Many times men are judged by their status and the amount of money they earn." Our Lord loves us all equally. He does not put a price tag on people and their worth. Remember, just as women want to be loved, men feel the need to be respected. When men are not shown respect they can become angry and then not forgive.

Method Three: The Love Languages

Another great way to communicate is through "The Love Languages", by Dr. Gary Chapman. He states that there are five ways people communicate. Many misunderstandings, assumptions, instances that cause hurt, anger and an inability to forgive, are rooted in not understanding the five love languages. I can say that the love languages have changed the way in which I understand others. They have been most helpful in my relationships with many people. The five love languages are words of affirmation, acts of service, receiving gifts, quality time and physical touch.

Words of affirmation; Words are spoken in order to tell others how much you care and love them. This is my love language. I love to tell people how important they are to me and how special they are. I love to write letters and encourage others in need.

Acts of Service; This is the love language in which someone you love will simply do special things for you. They will do service works such as clean your car or house, or do your laundry if you're sick.

Receiving Gifts; In this love language, you enjoy buying and giving gifts to others. It is a way to show care and love to another.

"A man's gift maketh room for him, and bringeth him before great men" (Proverbs 18:16). This is one of my love languages, what is yours?

Quality Time

This is the individual who would like to spend time with you. This is the person who will ask to go to an event just to be with you. If you don't attend the event, the other person may think you don't care. I have a family member who enjoys spending time with me and once stated that I did not care because I was not always available. Since this is not my love language, I was not sensitive to this person's feelings. After I read the book "The Love Languages" by Gary Chapman I understood that I needed to compromise and spend more time to show that I cared.

Physical Touch

Individuals feel loved when they hug another person, or shake hands. They may put their hand on another's shoulder to comfort a friend who is hurting. This is another of my favorite love languages.

I like to hug others and if someone does not hug me, I feel rejected. I remember a close friend of mine once stated I do not like to hug friends. I wanted to hug this person as a friendly gesture. At first I felt rejected and hurt. When I discovered the love languages, it helped me to understand and accept this behavior. It was a healing moment for me.

The love languages can apply to family, friends, co-workers and others who are in our lives. It does not only apply to those in romantic relationships. Everyone needs to be loved and accepted.

What is your love language?

Think about your love language for a moment. If someone had a different love language then you, did you judge, reject, or hold a grudge against them? Did you try to understand and communicate with them? Will you now be able to appreciate the different manners in which people express love as a gift from God? They are unique and so are you! Let us not concentrate on how different we are, instead let's focus on how we can relate to each other in a more loving and forgiving manner.

Number Five Action Step: Methods on how to communicate positively, and achieve forgiveness.

The Relaxation Method

Try this exercise every day this week, as a way of life;

Set up a relaxing time, with soft music playing, scented candles, and read the Bible or your favorite inspirational book. Have the mindset this week that you will put the love language skills into practice and communicate in a loving manner. Think of someone you may have held a grudge against and did not forgive because they didn't show love, or say the words you expected of them.

For the next week, go and make peace with them. You may want to tell them you want to have a better relationship with them. Practice talking to them about how the love languages can help improve communication between the both of you. Let us start today by treating everyone with respect and love. Let us understand one another and communicate with the best of others in mind. Let us, through forgiveness, save our relationships. We should look at and apply this to all of the important relationships in our lives; marriages, with our parents, kids, friends, and co-workers. With everyone we encounter. "Forgiving and being forgiven are two names for the same thing. The important thing is that it has been resolved."~ C.S. Lewis

Week Six: Forgiveness in Family, Friendships, and Co-worker Relationships

Forgiveness and Relationships

After Jesus, our relationships are one of the most precious gifts in our lives. We all have different DNA. Even twins, such as my twin sister Anna and I, are different. Jesus Our Lord taught us to forgive seventy times seven times. As the Holy Bible states, "Then came Peter to him, and said, Lord, how oft shall my brother sin against me, and I forgive him? Jesus saith unto him, I say not unto thee, Until seven times: but, Until seventy times seven. seventy times seven." (Matthew 18:21-22)

Are we more knowledgeable than our Lord in that we do not have to forgive others? This week we will talk about how to forgive family members, friends and co-workers. There will also be practical methods to keep our relationships healthy and forgiving.

Family Relationships

The traditional family has gone through many changes throughout the years. Single parenting and divorce are on the rise, as marriages are having a difficult time staying alive in our present culture. The Pew Institute researched relationships and found a record 40% of all households with children under the age of 18 include mothers who are either the sole or primary source of income for the family". The family unit is being broken up, which in turn causes a breakdown in society. Many incarcerated people in jail come from broken homes.

According to the American Psychological Association, "**Marriage and divorce** are both common experiences. In Western cultures, more than 90 percent of people marry by age 50. Healthy marriages are good for couple's mental and physical health. They are also good for children. Growing up in a happy home protects children from mental, physical, educational, and social problems. However, about 40 to 50 percent of married couples in the United States divorce." Look at the statistics. If we could forgive more often, would these statistics change? I believe they would. The next two methods that discuss how to forgive family members are, would you put yourself in my shoes, and pray together.

Method One: Forgiving Family Members

Would you put yourself in my shoes?
Five Questions to ask as you try to forgive family members. Try these exercises daily.

1. Was the offense done intentionally? If not, try to understand what the other person was experiencing, in order to understand their point of view and be able to communicate with them.

2. Were they under some unknown stress that you are unaware of? In a calm voice, and when tensions have lessened, ask them if something was bothering them.

3. Were they just having a bad day at the time, or were they tired and needed a rest? You may want to try to speak to them about what happened during a quieter time, or let it go.

4. Was there a miscommunication or misunderstanding? At a more peaceful time, ask the family member if you understood them, and clarify what you heard. It is best to verify that you understand them. Many times, problems arise between people because of a misunderstanding between the two parties.

5. Just remember, none of us are perfect and we all make mistakes. No one is perfect, and neither are you. Many times we expect others to always understand us, and we assume the worst. Some of our assumptions are incorrect and allow us the chance to find the truth in love. Take time to ask the family member for their side of the event. Give yourself, and them, a break.

Forgive

Method Two: Forgiving Family Members

Pray together

Pray together and it can change the course of problems and difficulties in our lives. It is difficult to hold onto anger when we pray together. Remember, our prayers and words can have a great effect on our lives.

"Be ye angry, and sin not: let not the sun go down upon your wrath: Neither give place to the devil." (Ephesians 4:26-27)

"Confess your faults one to another, and pray one for another, that ye may be healed. The effectual fervent prayer of a righteous man availeth much." (James 5:16)

Forgiving and Friendship

There are times when we may have an argument or disagreement with a friend, even a brother or sister in the Lord. We may be hurt, angry and experiencing shame or guilt. Our precious and special friends will disappoint us at times. How can we forgive from our heart? The Bible states, "A man that hath friends must shew himself friendly: and there is a friend that sticketh closer than a brother."(Proverbs 18:24)

It would be great to be, and find, friends like this. However, the real true friend who will never leave us or forsake us is Jesus. Humans are not perfect, and at times will fail us. Our Lord Jesus stated "And the Lord, he it is that doth go before thee; he will be with thee, he will not fail thee, neither forsake thee: fear not, neither be dismayed."(Deuteronomy 31:8.)

Our best friend is Jesus. He truly is the only one who will not leave you; Jesus will not discourage you, as humans too often do.

Many problems with friendship and forgiveness would be avoided if we would understand the qualities of what makes great friendships. Prevent problems in your relationships before they begin.

Seven Qualities of Great Friendships

1. In good times and bad, be available to just listen and understand. Be present with your friends.
2. Honesty

    Speak to your friend if he/she hurts you, and you feel it is hurting your relationship. You will not want to wait until the relationship is dissolved before you speak to your friend.
    "Faithful are the wounds of a friend; but the kisses of an enemy are deceitful." (Proverbs 27:6). Please be aware that you must speak honestly, with love and truth.
3. Humility

    Friends will listen to each other and respect each other's opinions without being defensive. A true friend can admit to his or her friend when they are wrong.
4. Giving

    A friend can give to another friend without having to give all of the time. Good friends can give laughter, acceptance, kindness, loyalty, and reach out during times of need and grief.
5. Show and Earn respect

    Show respect and ask your friend how they are feeling. Listen and understand. Accept their uniqueness, validate them, and show compassion.
6. Acceptance

    Accept a friend and appreciate their similarities, as well as their differences.
7. Encourage a friend and build them up, do not tear them down. Do not gossip or be critical. Be positive about life and the future. Demonstrate the Lord's unconditional love to your friends.

Forgiveness and Co-Workers

We spend a large majority of our time at work. Why is it that some people can get along at work, while others cannot? Why it is easy to talk to one co-worker, while others give us knots in our stomach. Some managers can be easy going while others are micromanagers. Some people frustrate and irritate us, while others are easy for us to accept. Why is it that we can laugh at one's person jokes and we might call someone else silly? Why do we hold grudges and harbor resentment against one co-worker, and others we do not. How can we learn to accept one another and be peaceful and forgiving in our work environment?

One method of helping individuals forgive in the work environment is to understand different personalities and temperaments. If you can think of each one of your co-workers as unique, gifted, talented and special, hopefully you can change to think of your irritating person at work as a friend you can learn something from. You can actually grow as a person. David Kiersey is known for his studies of personality and temperament. When you have an understanding of your personality and temperament, along with an understanding of other people's personalities and temperaments, you can view the beauty and differences of others as a gift to learn from, as opposed to them being frustrating and irritating people. Let us accept each other and live in forgiveness, even in our work environment.

One Method of Co-worker Forgiveness: Personality and Temperament

The four types of personality temperaments Kiersey named are the "Guardians, Idealists, Artisans, and the Rationalists." Guardians believe in law, order and respect for authority. They are dependable and have lots of fun with their friends. Idealists help people get along, and believe in working together. Conflict and confrontations upset them. Artisans are the artists, painters, sculptors and problem solvers. Rationalists will analyze and understand how things work better. They tend to tackle problems such as railroads, and computers.

Let's review how we can relate forgiveness to our places of work. Think of someone at work who irritates and frustrates you because they have a different temperament. We have resentment inside of us towards a co-worker who reacts differently to others than we do.

For example, a supervisor might have the temperament of a guardian. These individuals like order and dependability. They may not believe in socializing, thinking it gets in the way of us getting our work done. The idealist may do the work, but may take more time out to talk to co-workers to clarify work, or help other co-workers. The idealist may believe working together as a group will help production because people working in harmony produces more work than in an unfriendly atmosphere. Conflict between the guardian and the idealist may arise. The guardian may think the idealist is wasting company time by talking too much, while the idealist thinks it helps production when people socialize. Their point of view is that more is accomplished when people are working together in a less stressful and more peaceful environment. The guardian personality can appreciate that the idealist wants to make a positive change and bring harmony. The idealist can appreciate the importance of the guardian's desire to follow rules in order to maintain structure for the organization, to aid in job duties and tasks being completed efficiently. The guardian and idealist can learn and grow from each other's differences.

Think of your irritating person at work and forgive them. Look at them as being the person who the Lord created, and appreciate the gifts they have to offer to the world. Perhaps you can learn another way of doing things. The Bible states "Judge not, that ye be not judged. For with what judgment ye judge, ye shall be judged: and with what measure ye mete, it shall be measured to you again. And why beholdest thou the mote that is in thy brother's eye, but considerest not the beam that is in thine own eye? Or how wilt thou say to thy brother, Let me pull out the mote out of thine eye; and, behold, a beam is in thine own eye? Thou hypocrite, first cast out the beam out of thine own eye; and then shalt thou see clearly to cast out the mote out of thy brother's eye." (Matthew 7:1-5)

Remember, we are all wonderfully and beautifully created by the creator. Each one of us, even twins, has a different DNA and personality. How awesome! There is no one else on this earth that has the same DNA as you. Let us celebrate everyone around us. Let us not focus on our differences but how we are similar and how we can help one another. The Holy Bible states, ".I will praise thee; for I am fearfully and wonderfully made: marvellous are thy works; and that my soul knoweth right well." (Psalm139:14)

Number Six Action Step: Forgiveness, Relationships, Family, Friends and Co-Workers

During this week ask the Lord to show you how to forgive, and to be more understanding of the family, friends, co-workers or others who you have not forgiven. Spend some quiet time listening to our wonderful Lord give you peace in these relationships. Remember, you can only control yourself, not others.

Forgive Families

Think about who in your family you would like to forgive and why? Try putting yourself in their shoes.

Forgive Friends

Pray for guidance for the friends you would like to forgive and why. Why not be the best friend you can be, and call them or meet with them to discuss your differences? Read and practice the qualities of great friendships

Forgive Co-workers

Think of someone in your work place who irritates or frustrates you. It should be someone who you dislike because they have a different temperament than you. Pray for the strength to seek out co-workers who you can extend the hand of peace to, and be humble enough to discuss your differences with them. Forgive them. Offer to help them with a sincere heart. Offer to help with a project they are completing, or send a card either when they are sick or on their birthday. **Please let us not just talk about forgiveness, let us live it! It is freeing.** "Man has two great spiritual needs. One is for forgiveness. The other is for goodness." --Billy Graham

Week Seven: Methods on how to achieve forgiveness of the mind, body, and spirit.

Forgiveness and the Mind

Meditate about what you are telling yourself in all areas of your life; spiritual, family, friends, career, emotions, health, goals, and financial status. Are you thinking and acting in the character of Christ, which is forgiveness of others and self? Are you constantly telling yourself how fearful you are of asking for forgiveness? The Bible tells us to renew our minds and not be fearful. This includes not being afraid to forgive. You can apply the following scripture to your life and forgiveness.

"For God hath not given us the spirit of fear; but of power, and of love, and of a sound mind." (2: Timothy: 7)

"For who hath known the mind of the Lord, that he may instruct him? but we have the mind of Christ." (1 Corinthians 2:16)

"But the fruit of the Spirit is love, joy, peace, longsuffering, gentleness, goodness, faith, meekness, temperance: against such there is no law. And they that are Christ's have crucified the flesh with the affections and lusts. If we live in the Spirit, let us also walk in the Spirit." (Galatians 5: 22-25)

Some soul searching is required in order to ask the Lord to renew your mind to forgive. The Lord is for forgiveness and he is the one who can bring about true forgiveness and love in our minds and in our hearts. Please ask Jesus to show you His love. He is faithful and forgiving.

One Method of Forgiveness and the Mind

Inspirational thoughts for the mind to think about on forgiveness for different areas of your life; spiritual, career, emotions, health, great goals, and finances.

Spiritual- Keep connected to God because forgiveness is spiritual and God-like. It is spiritual to forgive another person for hurting us.

Career – If we are more fulfilled in our work and career, we are less likely to feel tired, irritated, and angry. Find a career you are passionate about and gifted in. It will hopefully keep you in a more forgiving and peaceful mood.

Emotions – Forgiveness will help to heal our emotions. It is beneficial to forgive.

Health – Forgiveness does help heal the physical being and keep us healthy and more peaceful. We only have one body, and we should take care of it.

Great Goals - Find great goals that you want for your life. Go out and try a new hobby, own a business, reconnect and spend more time with family and friends. Enjoy the present, because we can never get it back.

Financial Goals - Work together to resolve your differences concerning finances. One of the main problems in most marriages is related to finances. According to Katie Meyers "Seth Gilbert, How Financial Problems & Stress Cause Divorce, December 6, 2012, "You've probably heard that money problems are one of the most significant factors that can lead to a divorce. Without a doubt, differences in money management styles between two partners can ruin a marriage." Support, love, and forgiveness are especially needed during difficult financial situations such as unemployment and deciding how to resolve financial conflicts. Ask the Lord for the ability to forgive and provide for your needs. The Lord is faithful and will provide.

Forgiveness and the body

Forgiveness gives you these health benefits for your body.

One of the more significant benefits that you will gain from forgiveness is improved health. In his book "Forgive For Good", Dr. Fred Laskin cited a University of Wisconsin study that said, "learning to forgive may prevent heart disease in middle aged participants". In this study, the more the subjects showed a high level of forgiveness the fewer heart related problems they reported. At the same time, the more the participants reported a lack of forgiveness, the higher the frequency of heart issues."

The Bible addresses the benefits of forgiveness and peace in our lives. Being peaceful calms the whole body. It is as true now as it has ever been.

"Grace and peace be multiplied unto you through the knowledge of God, and of Jesus our Lord."
(2 Peter 1:2)

One may ask how someone can forgive those who murdered. Research completed in "Forgive for Good", on page 97 states, "Irish women showed an increase in forgiveness toward the person who committed the murder, of about 40 percent over the week of the training. This positive result remained constant at the follow up evaluation. Their depression scores also improved."

Method One: To keep your body healthy as you continue to forgive; Eat healthy

Eating healthy can help to become less susceptible to illness. As noted in the BJJ Scandinavia article, Acid Vs Alkaline, "To maintain health, the diet should consist of 60% alkaline forming foods and 40% acid forming foods. To restore health, the diet should consist of 80% alkaline forming foods and 20% acid forming foods..Generally, alkaline forming foods include: most fruits, green vegetables, peas, beans, lentils, spices, herbs, seasonings, seeds and nuts. .Generally, acid forming foods include: meat, fish, poultry, eggs, grains, and legumes".

Eating healthy can help our mind, body and spirit become more focused and less tired. If we are more focused and less tired, we are more likely to avoid misunderstanding, anger, and arguments. This in turn can cause us to become less bitter and more likely to forgive. As with any advice regarding physical health, it is best to first check with your personal physician.

Method Two: To keep your body healthy as you continue to forgive: Exercise

Many believe that we should exercise at least 20 minutes a day, three times a week or more. It will help you to feel alert and will assist in all around increased health and energy. If we are alive, vibrant and healthy, we are less likely to become agitated, angry and bitter towards others. It is recommended to please check with your doctor for the correct amount of exercise for you.

Method Three: To keep our body healthy as you continue to forgive: Proper Rest

Allow yourself time to sleep without disturbance and with a clear mind. Close down the bitter thoughts for the day, and allow the Lord to give you a peaceful sleep. As (Psalm 4:8) says, "I will both lay me down in peace, and sleep: for thou, Lord, only makest me dwell in safety."

There are many prayer lines to call to talk to someone twenty four hours a day, seven days a week if you are struggling in forgiving others. I have called these prayer lines on many occasions. They are free and I have spoken to some of the most compassionate, understanding caring individuals to help get through difficult times.

One Method to Achieve Forgiveness in the Spirit: Prayer

Forgiveness and the Spirit

Forgiveness is one of the most spiritual things we can do for ourselves and others. The Our Father states in the bible, (Matthew 6:12), "And forgive us our debts, as we forgive our debtors." When saying these words, we are tapping into the spiritual world, which helps give us the ability to forgive others when we are unable to do so on our own. There is tremendous freedom in forgiveness

Prayer

Praying to God can help us forgive others. Prayer is talking to God about how we feel towards someone or something. God will give us the answers. Research proves that prayer is effective in helping us to be forgiven, and to forgive others. It takes the supernatural spiritual power of God for us to receive the miracle of forgiveness. Some would ask how to pray to forgive someone who has hurt us tremendously. Prayer is truly good for the spirit and soul

In the article, 'Power of Prayer: Studies Find Prayer Can Lead to Cooperation, Forgiveness in Relationships': "Participants who prayed for a close relationship partner on days in which conflict occurred reported higher levels of cooperative tendencies and forgiveness than on days when conflict occurred and they did not pray."

Another prayer study, entitled "Discussing Spirituality with Patients", found the following: "Patient spirituality and religiosity have been shown to be correlated with reduced morbidity and mortality, better physical and mental health, healthier lifestyles, fewer required health services, improved coping skills, enhanced well-being, reduced stress, and illness.

Similarly, in "Prayer: What is Prayer", it is documented that hope, belief, and faith positively influence health outcomes.

Research proves that people who pray are healthier, have happier lives and heal quicker. In my personal journey the power of prayer has healed broken relationships, provided physical and emotional healing, and has lessened the difficultly of being unemployed. Tap into something greater than yourself; Prayer.

Number Seven Action Step: Methods on how to achieve forgiveness of the mind, body, and spirit.

Forgiveness and the Mind

Practice forgiveness techniques of the mind on a daily basis to stay in forgiveness. When you are feeling anger towards a loved one, breathe and inhale. Ask the Lord to help you relax and find peace. Think to yourself; is this the right time and place to discuss my anger? Will it benefit and help heal the situation?

During your quiet, relaxed time, ask yourself what you can do to resolve your difficulty and anger. Make sure to remind yourself to not assume anything from anybody. Think the best before you make a negative assumption about someone. As the Bible states in (Second Timothy 1:7) "For God hath not given us the spirit of fear; but of power, and of love, and of a sound mind." (Philippians 4:8) states, "Finally, brethren, whatsoever things are true, whatsoever things are honest, whatsoever things are just, whatsoever things are pure, whatsoever things are lovely, whatsoever things are of good report; if there be any virtue, and if there be any praise, think on these things."

Forgiveness and the Body

Eating well ,exercise and proper rest should become a part of your life on a regular basis. Organic foods can be a great aid in eating well. Please check with your doctor to best determine an exercise plan that fits your specific needs.

Forgiveness and the Spirit

Try praying for one week, or longer, about a situation, and ask the Lord to help you forgive someone. The power of prayer in action will amaze you.

Please find a list of prayers to pray and ask for forgiveness. Let us take some quiet time to pray. Please read the inspirational guide "How to Stay in Forgiveness Daily" listed in week seven. Remember the words contained in this guide when you are feeling stressed about something, or want to fall back into resentment and not forgive. Ask Jesus to show you how to forgive others. Ask Jesus to come into your heart to change your bitterness to love. Ask Jesus to be your Savior. The Lord changed my life when I asked him to be my Savior

Remember, "Be it known unto you therefore, men and brethren, that through this man is preached unto you the forgiveness of sins: And by him all that believe are justified from all things, from which ye could not be .justified by the law of Moses" (Acts 13:38-39).

"There was a man of the Pharisees, named Nicodemus, a ruler of the Jews: The same came to Jesus by night, and said unto him, Rabbi, we know that thou art a teacher come from God: for no man can do these miracles that thou doest, except God be with him. Jesus answered and said unto him, Verily, verily, I say unto thee, Except a man be born again, he cannot see the kingdom of God. Nicodemus saith unto him, How can a man be born when he is old? can he enter the second time into his mother's womb, and be born? Jesus answered, Verily, verily, I say unto thee, Except a man be born of water and of the Spirit, he cannot enter into the kingdom of God. That which is born of the flesh is flesh; and that which is born of the Spirit is spirit. Marvel not that I said unto thee, Ye must be born again. The wind bloweth where it listeth, and thou hearest the sound thereof, but canst not tell whence it cometh, and whither it goeth: so is every one that is born of the Spirit. Nicodemus answered and said unto him, How can these things be? Jesus answered and said unto him, Art thou a master of Israel, and knowest not these things? Verily, verily, I say unto thee, We speak that we do know, and testify that we have seen; and ye receive not our witness. If I have told you earthly things, and ye believe not, how shall ye believe, if I tell you of heavenly things? And no man hath ascended up to heaven, but he that came down from heaven, even the Son of man which is in heaven. And as Moses lifted up the serpent in the wilderness, even so must the Son of man be lifted up: That whosoever believeth in him should not perish, but have eternal life. For God so loved the world, that he gave his only begotten Son, that whosoever believeth in him should not perish, but have everlasting life. For God sent not his Son into the world to condemn the world; but that the world through him might be saved."

(John 3:1-17)

How to Stay in Forgiveness

1. Pray first to receive the understanding of others.
2. Think before you speak.
3. Listen twice as much as you talk.
4. Don't assume /Ask.
5. Be Positive towards others.
6. Forgive for you and others.
7. Don't go to bed angry.
8. Apologize.
9. Be the peacemaker. Each day find someone to bless, call someone in need or just bring flowers, food, or help to a homeless person. Do something nice.
10. Be kind to those you have not forgiven.
11. Be grateful for all your blessings from the Lord. On a daily basis remind yourself of one thing you have to be grateful for.
12. Ask for clarification if you don't understand.
13. Do not ignore others when frustrated, instead ask for clarification and understanding.
14. Life is short, make every day count.
15. Tell someone you love them.

Closing Thoughts on Beyond Second Chances

I'd like to close with two important thoughts about forgiveness from a bible scripture and a Christian song, which won a Dove award in 1996, "Just between You and Me" by DC Talk.

It is said in (Ephesians 4:29-32); "Let no corrupt communication proceed out of your mouth, but that which is good to the use of edifying, that it may minister grace unto the hearers. And grieve not the Holy Spirit of God, whereby ye are sealed unto the day of redemption. Let all bitterness, and wrath, and anger, and clamor, and evil speaking, be put away from you, with all malice: And be ye kind one to another, tenderhearted, forgiving one another, even as God for Christ's sake hath forgiven you."

It would be a fantastic manner in which to live as Ephesians 4:29 mentions. Our world would be a much more peaceful place.

My favorite lyric regarding forgiveness is wonderful, and it states, "If confession is the road to healing, forgiveness is the promised land."

Thank you for being part of the Beyond Second Chances forgiveness program. I am honored that you have taken the time to share my passion and journey about forgiveness.

My hope is The Beyond Second Chances forgiveness training program will be life changing. Your life with the Lord, others and yourself will never be the same. You will be become more loving, forgiving, and open, which will hopefully lead to lasting freedom of your mind, body and spirit.

The Forgiveness House

It has been a dream of mine to develop a house where individuals can go on a retreat to relax and enjoy the beauty of our world through nature, trees and fresh air. A place where one can have times of silence with the Lord, laughter, fellowship, love, acceptance, and just plain fun. The house I envision would be in New Hampshire near the White Mountains. It would be open from July through October, because I would like to spend the rest of the year there with my family and friends.

When the Forgiveness House is open, it would be a retreat house to teach the principles of the Beyond Second Chances program,. This seminar would teach the principles of the program all day Saturday from 9 to 5, and Sunday morning after church for a few hours.

My prayer is that the principles taught about forgiveness will save marriages, families, single parents, people who are single, those with addictions, mental illness, anxiety, depression, or any other person who struggles with not being able to forgive. There would be weekends reserved for specific individuals, such as couples, families, seniors, singles, the mentally ill, those with chemical dependencies, educators, life coaches, social workers and counselors.

There would be accommodations for about 100 people per weekend. We may have food catered, or go out, depending on individual preferences. The house would be set in the mountains with beautiful cottages, a swimming pool, a spa, and a conference center. Christian worship music would be part of the entire week. The cost to run the Forgiveness House would be minimal, and would be funded by donations from individuals, Christian non-profits, corporations, and churches. There would also be a large sign in the Conference Center stating, "No one is a Loser. We are just broken people who can be healed through the Lord, Love and Forgiveness"

Beyond Second Chances Website/To Be Free /Weekly Blog/The Power of Forgiveness

If you are interested in staying connected with the Beyond Second Chances training, please visit our website at beyondsecondchances.net. List your name, email address, and phone number for future Beyond Second Chances forgiveness events and workshops. Each week I will be adding to the "To Be Free" section of the Beyond Second Chances website. This is a weekly inspirational thought of the week on forgiveness and how to stay peaceful in our sometimes chaotic world.

In a weekly blog I will answer your questions on forgiveness, plus discuss, inspire, and educate on the power of forgiveness. Soon thereafter there will be forgiveness training programs in your community, forgiveness training teacher's manuals and videos. In addition there will also be To Be Free Forgiveness inspirational series, your children's forgiveness books, and Christian Soaking music to calm the weary soul.

Thank you for sharing this time together.

Love, Forgiveness, and Blessings,
Carol Rolleri
Forgiveness Trainer for Beyond Second Chances

Notes

1. Your Dictionary The Dictionary you can understand: American Heritage Dictionary: Forgiveness. Retrieved from the American Heritage website: Your dictionary.com
2. Howes, R. (2010, January, 27). In Therapy, A user's guide to psychotherapy, Cool intervention #9, The Empty Chair. Psychology today. Retrieved from the website: http://www.psychologytoday.com/blog/in-therapy/201001/cool-intervention-9-the-empty-chair-1
3. Encyclopedia of Psychology: 8 Volume Set Alan E. Kazdin, PhD, Editor-in-Chief Retrieved from the American Psychological Association website: http://www.apa.org/topics/divorce/index.aspx Kazdin (2000)
4. Kiersey.com:http:/website/www.keirsey.com/4temps/guardian_overview.asp.Please Understand Me II: Temperament Character Intelligence David Keirsey, Prometheus Nemesis Book Company Del Mar, CA, 1998.
5. Gilbert, K & Meyers, S (December 6, 2012) How Financial Problems & Stress Cause Divorce. Psychology Today/Insight is 20/20. Website: Psychologyhttp://www.psychologytoday.com/blog/insight-is-2020/201212/how-financial-problems-stress-cause-divorce. (Gilbert & Meyers 2012).
6. Laskin, F. 2002. Forgive for Good: A Proven Prescription for Health and Happiness. New York, N.Y. Harper Collins Publisher Page 87 and 97 Laskin (2002).
7. BJJ Scandinavia Acidic Vs. Alkaline. (January, 19, 2014) essence of Life FoodsWebsite:http://www.bjjscandinavia.com/2014/01/19/acidic-vs-alkaline-foods/BJJ Scandinavia and Grappling News Lifestyle in Scandinavia. (January 19, 2014).
8. Elish, J (May 2013) Power of Prayer: Studies Find Prayer Can Lead to Cooperation, Forgiveness in Relationships Released: 14-May-2013 / Florida State University/Jill Elish May 2013
9. Website: http://www.newswise.com/articles/power-of-prayer-studies-find-prayer-can-lead-to-cooperation-forgiveness-in-relationships
10. McCord, G (July 2004) Discussing Spirituality With Patients: A Rational and Ethical Approach, (Gary McCord), MA, Department of Family Medicine, Northeastern Ohio Universities College of Medicine, Rootstown, Ohio. Website http://www.ncbi.nlm.nih.gov/pmc/articles/PMC1466687/ US National Library of Medicine, (July, 2004)

11. Prayer: Prayer What is Prayer / Created for Spirituality and Healing 2014 Regents of the University of Minnesota and Charlson The University of Minnesota is an equal opportunity educator and employer.(October 31, 2013) Website http://www.takingcharge.csh.umn.edu/explore-healing-practices/prayer
12. D.C. Talk: Just Between You and Me Retrieved on the website: www.lyricsFreak.com/d/dc+talk/between+you+ME20037682.HTML.

Bibliography

American Heritage Dictionary: forgiveness: Retrieved from the website ahdictionary.com

BJJ Scandinavia Acidic Vs. Alkaline. (January, 19, 2014) essence of Life Foods Website:http://www.bjjscandinavia.com/2014/01/19/acidic-vs-alkaline-foods/BJJ Scandinavia and Grappling News Lifestyle in Scandinavia. (January 19, 2014).

Breadwinner Moms: Mothers Are the Sole or Primary Provider in Four-in-Ten Households with Children; Public Conflicted about the Growing trends. www.pewsocialtrends.org/2013/05/29/breadwinner-moms

Chapman, G (1992, 1995, 2004, 2010). The 5 Love Languages: The Secret to Love that Lasts. Chicago, Ill: Northfield Publishers

Doheny, Kathleen: Pets for Depression and Health WebMD. Retrieved from the website www.webmd.com/depression/features/pets-depression

Eggerich, Emerson. (2004). The Love She Desires the Most and the Respect He Desperately Needs. Nashville, Tenn: Thomas Nelson

Elish, J (May 2013) Power of Prayer: Studies Find Prayer Can Lead to Cooperation, Forgiveness in Relationships Released: 14-May-2013 / Florida State University/Jill Elish May 2013.
Website http://www.newswise.com/articles/power-of-prayer-studies-find-prayer-can-lead-to-cooperation-forgiveness-in-relationships

Encyclopedia of Psychology: 8 Volume Set: Alan E. Kazdin, PhD, Editor-in-Chief American Psychological Association: websitettp://www.apa.org/topics/divorce/index.aspx: Kazdin, (2000)

Gilbert, K & Meyers, S (December 6, 2012) How Financial Problems & Stress Cause Divorce. Psychology Today/Insight is 20/20.

Harris, Guy. (2006). "Listen More, Speak Less - 5 Steps to Better Listening" Retrieved on the website: http:WWW.INSIDE.

Kiersey.com:http:/website:/www.keirsey.com/4temps/guardian_overview.as.Please Understand Me II: Temperament Character Intelligence. David Keirsey, Prometheus Nemesis Book Company. Del Mar, CA, 1998.

Laskin, F. 2002. Forgive for Good: A Proven Prescription for Health and Happiness. New York, N.Y. Harper Collins Publisher Page 87 and 97 Laskin (2002).

McCord, G (July 2004) Discussing Spirituality With Patients: A Rational and Ethical Approach, (Gary McCord), MA, Department of Family Medicine, Northeastern Ohio Universities College of Medicine, Rootstown, Ohio. Website http://www.ncbi.nlm.nih.gov/pmc/articles/PMC1466687/ US National Library of Medicine, (July, 2004)

Merriam-Webster Dictionary and Thesaurus communication and respect Retrieved from the website: www.merriam-webster.com

Phoenix, G.R. . . .How To Love A Woman. Phoenix, G.R. G (2011, February). Retrieved from the website, grahamreid.com/2011/02/10-ways-to-love.

Prayer: Prayer What is Prayer / Created for Spirituality and Healing 2014 Regents of the University of Minnesota and Charlson The University of Minnesota is an equal opportunity educator and employer.(October 31, 2013) Website http://www.takingcharge.csh.umn.edu/explore-healing-practices/prayer

Pew website Pew Research and Social and Demographic Trends (May 29, 2013).http: Scott, E. (2011 Oct 27). "How music affects us and why music therapy promotes health" MS

Scott, Elizabeth: Music and your Body: How music affects us and why music therapy promotes health. Retrieved from the website: http://www.webmd.com/depression/features/pets-depression

Stanley, Charles: Victory Over Rejection; October 17, 2013http://www.youtube.com/watch?v=tAvQfsItyWA

The Benefits We Experience When Animals Are Beside Us. Retrieved from the website www.holisticonline.com/stress/stress-pet-therapy-benefits-of-pets-htm

About the Author

Caroline Rolleri has a Masters of Social Work from Rutgers University, and is a licensed social worker and forgiveness trainer in New Jersey. She has provided mental health counseling, case management, and social services to thousands of individuals, in settings such as in-patient psychiatric hospitals, out-patient clinics, state facilities, community programs, and the health care industry. She has provided one-on-one counseling, group therapy and didactic groups to individuals who were elderly, homeless, unemployed, addicted, single parents, divorced, and suffering from anxiety or depression.

She has experienced dramatic healing from anxiety and depression through the power of forgiveness. After this experience she developed Beyond Second Chances, an innovative seven week program for the mind and body, which espouses the spiritual power of forgiveness. Passionate about healing the hurting, her dream is to help the hurting heal by learning the gift of forgiveness. She would also like to open a Forgiveness House, a place where individuals, groups and educators can get together to learn the Beyond Second Chances forgiveness program, and share it with their families, friends, co-workers, churches, schools and communities.

Quote from Mother Theresa

"When a poor person dies of hunger, it has not happened because God did not take care of him or her. It has happened because neither you nor I wanted to give that person what he or she needed."

"I pray that you will understand the words of Jesus, "Love one another as I have loved you." Ask yourself "How has he loved me? Do I really love others in the same way?" Unless this love is among us, we can kill ourselves with work and it will only be work, not love. Work without love is slavery."

www.ingramcontent.com/pod-product-compliance
Lightning Source LLC
Chambersburg PA
CBHW080534030426
42337CB00023B/4737